Reflections of a Soul's Journey

魂の旅の映像

PETER J. PRATO, PhD

Noble House
Baltimore, Maryland

Reflections of a Soul's Journey
魂の旅の映像

Copyright © 1995 Peter J. Prato, PhD

Artwork by *Sakai*

Library of Congress
Cataloging in Publication Data
ISBN 1-56167-216-5
Library of Congress Card Catalog Number:
95-069932

Published by

8019 Belair Road, Suite 10
Baltimore, Maryland 21236

Manufactured in the United States of America

Dedication

This book of poetry is dedicated to the memory of my sister Betty and my former wife Janice, who look down from a spiritual place somewhere on this book with a smile, and to my son Steve and my daughter Liz, both of whom I know to be eternal companions and who, in this life time, have helped me to know the meaning of unconditional love.

Tao

The Tao that can be told is not the eternal Tao.
The name that can be named is not the eternal name.
The nameless is the beginning of heaven and earth.
The named is the mother of ten thousand things.
Ever desireless, one can see the mystery.
Ever desiring, one can see the manifestations.
These two spring from the same source but differ in name;
       this appears as darkness.
Darkness within darkness.
The gate to all mystery.

Feng, Sia-Fu and Jane English. <u>Tao Te Ching, Translation</u>. New York: Vantage Books, Random House. p. 1.

PROLOGUE

As human consciousness and understanding evolve and expand, it becomes more and more apparent that humankind is destined to travel a pathway of ever increasing spiritual awareness.

Pierre Teilhard de Chardin, renowned Jesuit philosopher and paleontologist, wrote in his epic work *The Phenomenon of Man* that an individual could use his free will to be in harmony with a Universal Intelligence and thus step beyond the physical process of evolution. Teilhard was among the first to recognize that the path of human evolution had become a way to higher consciousness and spirituality. Later in *The Divine Milieu* he revealed how, through spiritual awakening, we can become "participants in the destiny of the universe."

Eminent thinkers throughout the world are increasingly coming to embrace this spiritual philosophy. Carl Jung, perhaps this century's most creative psychologist, in concert with Teilhard's thinking, recognized that science and psychology had reached the frontier of a totally unified world, the *unas mundas*. The discoveries of modern physics reveal a universe of dynamic underlying unity where all things, events, and individuals are related and influenced by a Wisdom of unimaginable magnitude. This unitary world view, which embraced all life and human activities, Jung realized had an ever deepening affinity with the world view of Chinese philosophy. At its heart is a single governing principle—the Tao. The concept of Tao literally means path or way which leads from a beginning directly to a goal. According to Richard Wilhelm, the late distinguished sinologist, "the Tao, although in itself motionless, is the source of all motion. . .the whole of all activity in nature and the universe, visible and invisible, is governed by a single principle, the Tao."

The way of the Tao is spiritual—a journey to ever increasing levels of spiritual understanding—a pathway that Jung labeled the process of individuation.

The call for individuation—for the expansion of consciousness and spiritual awareness—thus arises from our deepest Source of Life. This Source strives unceasingly to bring about the realization in our lives that we have a unique spiritual pathway that arises through the unconscious mind—through our dreams, intuition, joys, and sufferings, and directs us to become what we were *meant* to become. For Jung, this process revealed an "immediate religious experience that lead ultimately to a highly personalized spiritual wholeness."

Much earlier Meister Eckhart (1260-1329), eminent Dominican priest, philosopher, and mystic, intuitively described this process when he wrote:

Know that all creatures are driven and take action by their nature for one end; to be like God. Heaven would never revolve if it did not search for God or a likeness of God. If God were not in all things, nature would not accomplish or yearn for anything . . . For whether you wish it or not and whether you know it or not, within itself, nature seeks and strives for God.

For Eckhart, humanity was a likeness of the Divine that has no parallel: "The soul is destined to such a great and noble good. . .The soul must always hurry to this goal, that it can by every means come to the eternal good that is God— it is for this that the soul was created." *

* Fox, Matthew. *Breakthrough: Meister Eckhart's Creation Spirituality*. New York: Doubleday Dell Publishing Group, Inc., 1991. 63-107.

Through his poetry, Peter accesses the deep and sensitive areas in the psyche that Jung called "primordial images or archetypes" which, because of their universality and antiquity, possess a cosmic and superhuman character. His poetry emerges from his efforts to experience and understand these ancient promptings from his unconscious mind. Thus he gifts us with the inspiration received when communication has been distinctly made with the mystical knowing many call the Soul. We, however, are left free to interpret the written universal theme found within each poem for ourselves. In this way Peter's poetry gives meaning and unity to many of the feelings and sensations that are a part of our life experience and provides us with a pathway through which we can bring our intuitive thoughts and experiences into conscious awareness.

Rita Lynn, Ph.D.
Pleasanton, CA

Table of Contents

Prologue   v

Tao   1
An Eternal Thought   3
Find God Within—God Without   4
Amazing   5
God Is Not a Butterfly   6
I Am   7
Magnificent   8
There is the Presence . . .   9
A Pretty Petal   10
Looking Over My Shoulder   11
Pleroma   12
Harmonic Convergence   13

Evolved Individuals   15
In the Common Time   17
The Greatest Miracle of All   18
A Personal Everest   19
A Scholar's Wisdom   20
Evolution   21
Of the Universal Law   22
To err is human . . .   23
Tuned to the Vibrations of the Universe   24
Restore Honor to Business   26
Shodan (Karate)   28
Universal Protection   29
No Greater Gift   30
When I Look   31
Tide   32
Making Sense   33
The Way   34
Killing one person . . .   35
A Divine Resplendency   36

There is the Presence . . .   37
Suffering . . .   38
Time   39
This Instant   40
Reunion   41
Cast Your Nets to the Right   42
Our Emotional Nature   43
Affirm the negatives . . .   44
A Man's Immortality   45
Life   46
Another Way   47
The Endlessness of Me   48
My True Power   49
True Freedom   50
Spend time with yourself . . .   51
Tears   52
Tears wash away . . .   53
I Had a Dream   54
Night Child   55
To My Dog Rex   57
Acceptance   59
An Ode to a Son and to a Father   60
A Spiritual Family   61
Who Is This Man?   62
Some Coaches   64

The Evolving Tao   67
A Different Way   69
Grace   70
A Warrior's Last Call   71
A Journey of Love   73
On the Journey of Life   74
The presence of God . . .   75
A Transitional Prayer   76
A Free Spirit   77
A Voice for Men to Hear   78
What Is the Purpose?   79

A Universal Wind   81

Unconditional Love   83
Unconditional Love   85
To Know Love   86
Love Is an Act   87
Love Is a Verb   88
I Did It My Way   89
Is It Better?   90
Each Spring   91
Anima   92
Soul Mate   93
An Awakening   95
I Must Move On   96
Because of you . . .   98
The capacity to love . . .   99
The Light of Love   100
Love You from a Distance   101
Something that everyone dreams of . . .   103
Kindred Spirit   104
Love is like a ray . . .   105
Sometimes Soul Mates Do Not Meet   106
A Memory   108
Learn to be vulnerable . . .   109
Love is like a flower . . .   110

Nature   111
Chrysalis   113
A Flower   114
Beauty   115
The dawn leaves me . . .   116
A Search for Wholeness   117
A Sunset   119
A dream is a vision . . .   120
Snow   121

Death   123
The Ultimate Reality   125
I Free Thee (and me)   126
To my Grandmother (A Soliloquy)   127
Grandmother (A Revelation)   128
Tasha (A Remembrance)   130
Expectation   131
Confrontation   132
Sometimes we forget . . .   133
At Death   134
A Journey   135
Death   136

Epilogue   137

Tao

Unknowable   Unfathomable   Mysterious
The Source of Ten Thousand Things

AN ETERNAL THOUGHT

Perhaps a Pantheist would fully know,
What I have slowly come to see,
That the Universal Purpose,
May be fully revealed in a tree.

When God began the universe an eternity ago,
A tree could only have been something—
Only He could know.

Amid the gases, molecules and vast diversity,
A thought was born that formed a tree,
As it stands there—majestically.

In the time it took from then 'til now,
While the universe was cast,
Stars were made—and some have gone,
Infinite time has passed.

But a tree was always meant to be,
So magnificently wrought
It is now—as it was then,
God's eternal thought.

FIND
GOD WITHIN—GOD WITHOUT

Some say,
Seek the God within—
To find the source of mind's milieu;
And the inner search,
To find our source,
Is valid, just and true.

As we go within,
We find our soul,
Our flesh declines,
Our spirit rings with bliss,
And somehow we know deep within,
We've touched the power of God in this.

It is wonderful to know this bliss,
This sacred inner chime,
And when we ring this sacred bell,
In a mystery sublime,
It rings a mighty outer bell,
In perfect chord and time.

In God within and God without,
A perfect balance be—
Our inner ringing of this bell,
Resonates God's outer symphony.

AMAZING

It is amazing,
That the great power,
That fills the universe with order,
And love and joy—
And seems to be preoccupied,
On a magnificent scale,
With the series of events,
That are being created everywhere,
By everyone and everything—
Can take the time,
Sometime,
When I allow,
To touch and fill my soul,
With courage, warmth,
And love.

GOD IS NOT A BUTTERFLY

God is not a butterfly,
That flits from flower to tree,
God is like the radiant sun,
Which warms us endlessly.

Lord, give me the strength to rise above,
The illusions of the hour,
That say Your love is momentary,
And has very little power.

Give me the strength to know,
Your touch is always there;
Give me the wisdom to understand
It fills me everywhere.

No, God is not a butterfly,
That flits from flower to tree,
God is the Universal Message,
"I am always there with thee."

I AM

I spoke a question to the Universe.
I asked that Presence that my mind,
Cannot fully comprehend,
To identify itself to me.
An inner voice spoke:
I am the absence of any substance,
Contained within the all of all substance;
I am the sky and the earth,
The good and the absence of good,
The microcosm and the
Macrocosm,
The pace of a snail,
And the speed of light;
I am the good in all,
And the absence of the good in all,
I am the idea and the manifestation,
The amorphous,
And the solid form,
I am love,
And the absence of love,
I am Spirit,
And groundedness,
I am yin,
And I am yang,
I am all and,
Everywhere in all.
I Am.

MAGNIFICENT

God must be made of magnificent stuff,
Of light,
So radiant and pure,
Of truth and hope and gentleness;
Of love,
So sensitive, caring and sublime.
Of strength and loving power too,
To shape the heavens afar,
And move them in their perfect paths forever.
Magnificent.

There is the Presence of God in every man.

"Is it not written in your law that Ye are Gods—
Sons of God most high?"

A PRETTY PETAL

A pretty petal drifting up,
From deep within a vase,
Your brief purpose now is to adorn.
Tomorrow dawns and wonders,
Where has that pretty flower gone?

Each petal touched with wonderment,
And beauty of design,
A touch of brown,
A speck of yellow,
A center of pure gold,
Some buds that have not yet expressed,
The beauty you enfold.

How can we look at you,
And only come to see,
An ornament—within a vase—
An object of beauty.

More than this you surely are,
Oh splendid little thing,
God's creation flows from you,
Your life a song to sing.

Your beauty, severed at the root,
Must now ebb from you,
No matter—this is not the end,
The Universe permits each flower,
To bloom and bloom again.

LOOKING OVER
MY SHOULDER

Lord, forgive me for looking back over my shoulder,
When it's time for me to thank You.
Forgive me for often forgetting,
The loving things that You do.

It's easy to cry out, Lord! Lord!
When I'm troubled and gripped with pain.
How simple it is to forget You,
When Your love erases the strain.

After I solve a life problem,
And am enchanted by what I have done,
It's easy to forget that Your Presence,
Underlies each deed under the sun.

So forgive me for looking over my shoulder,
As is human to often do,
When it seems for an unthinking moment,
I did it myself without You.

PLEROMA

It was said by poets
And wisemen of old,
That man is the essence
Of all God enfolds,
In the Universe.

If we could grasp a distant star,
And pluck a tiny piece,
Of that star's fundamental flame;
The unit that we held,
Would reflect in every way,
The essence of the star,
From which it came.

This thought speaks to us,
Because we each contain,
The essence of the loving Source,
From which we all came.

This great creative Source,
Is implicit in each cell,
In protons and electrons,
And in every ocean swell.

God is surely here with us,
A part of all we are;
In every human being,
In every grain of sand,
In all things,
In the Universe.

HARMONIC CONVERGENCE

At this time
In the infinite history of the universe,
A Universal Good
Has caused an energy of Love to flow.
As it pervades,
The vast expanse of space,
It causes stars,
And planets,
To constellate,
In a different way.
This magnificent Presence
Also touches planet Earth
And enters into the spirit,
Of each rock,
Rill,
Each flower,
And hill;
And simultaneously,
Finds its way into,
The hearts and souls of all of us,
To some degree or other.
And then this love begins to spread,
To friend and foe alike,
In the universal family,
And
As this Love penetrates our souls,
Upon our lips and in our hearts,
There slowly forms a single word,
Peace.

Evolved Individuals
Truth　　　Life　　　Family

IN THE COMMON TIME

Lord, teach me to love in the common time,
In the empty time in life;
Teach me to love when there's hurt and woe,
And my heart is filled with strife.

Lord, it's easy to love at Christmas time,
When the lights reflect man's cheer;
Teach me to love in the other times,
When there are no chimes to hear.

Teach me to love when there's misery,
When my spirit's sad and low;
Teach me to love when there's hatred,
When my anger's all aglow.

Teach me to love when there's sadness,
When it seems so hard to try;
It's easy to love when there's gladness,
When the spirit's crest is high.

Lord, teach me to love as You do,
When life's tenor has no rhyme;
Let the bliss of Your love guide me,
In the empty common time.

THE GREATEST
MIRACLE OF ALL

There is a miraculous quality in nature,
That man can feel and see,
An endless stream of truth and beauty,
That reveals itself splendidly.

In the workings of the atom,
Each electron held in perfect symmetry,
By a force expressing order,
A radiant mystery.

Take the lowly, simple acorn,
Cut apart does not reveal a tree;
Yet implicit in this acorn,
A tree! A perfect tree to be.

Look upon the migrant sea gull,
Who flies over the endless, uncharted sea;
Without the aid of chart or compass,
Arriving at its destination errorlessly.

See the harmony in the universe,
A symphony beyond compare,
Each star in perpetual order,
Perfection everywhere!

Look beyond this to your neighbor,
As he listens for God's loving call,
Deep within his mortal being lives,
Natures greatest miracle of all!

A PERSONAL EVEREST

I set out to climb a mountain,
A rugged mountain high;
I struggled, clutched and fought with it,
It seemed to reach the sky.

I tried again to scale its height,
To win my victory;
The mountain only seemed to grow,
A towering sight to see.

Again I tried its craggy side,
And commanded it retreat!
The mountain's strength increased tenfold,
It sent me to defeat.

I paused to seek an Inner Source,
My soul a strength to find;
A thought came forth from deep within,
It filled my heart and mind.

Bigger than it is right now,
That mount could never be,
This revelation swells my strength,
The growth will be in me.

(Dedicated to Gerry Mulhall who gave me the inspiring theme for this poem.)

A SCHOLAR'S WISDOM

An aged scholar said,
When asked by men of might;
Where should I go? What should I do?
Whose ethics make things right?

If you should look to other men,
To tell you what to do,
You miss the mark—the scholar said,
Truth's arrow flies not true.

Before you look to other men,
Your conduct to make clear,
Look deep within yourself—my son,
Your own voice of truth to hear.

Truth's voice resides in every man,
Alas, it's there in you;
Be guided by this voice of truth,
In all things that you do.

EVOLUTION

If the Soul of man be so immortal,
Why is it encased in flesh and limb?
If the Soul can transcend oceans,
Why must man be taught to swim?

If the Soul is so immortal,
What leads man to often err?
Why does immortality seek,
A companion in despair?

What was the strange coincidence,
That placed the Spirit in,
The frailty of humanity—
Often—disposed to sin?

Surely we were touched,
By this inner sanctity,
To draw our vision up to God,
To sense our destiny.

For Spirit comes to know its essence,
Within the flesh it seems to be,
Ever seeking—ever learning—
On its path toward God—Infinity.

OF THE UNIVERSAL LAW

Know these things in life situations.
You can be in tune with the laws of man,
But in that attunement, you cannot violate the Laws of God.
The Laws of God are laws of Love—Truth—
Compassion and Justice.
They stifle and overpower,
Acts of injustice and discrimination.

This is the truth.
Where there is no love and compassion,
there exists a vacuum,
That soon fills with suffering and desolation.
You cannot be unjust and expect justice.
You cannot be unkind and expect kindness.
You cannot be cruel and expect compassion.
You cannot be dishonest and expect honest conduct
to be returned to you.
You cannot lie and expect the truth.
You cannot deceive your neighbor and expect
to reap his blessing.
You cannot cheat and expect life to reward you.
You cannot hate and expect love—
As you sow, so shall you reap.

These are laws that govern life's situations;
They are God's laws—they transcend the laws of men.

To err is human,
Forgive divine—
Is Truth.

TUNED TO THE VIBRATIONS
OF THE UNIVERSE

There is an energy of death,
And an energy of Life,
In everyone.
Witness how they work;
In youth the energy of Life,
Is strong
And vibrant
Because the child is totally trusting,
Of the Universal Good.

As we grow older the trials and crises of life,
Often cloud this energy,
And create states of disharmony,
From our hatred, anger, scorn,
Unforgiveness and disbelief . . .

And when we begin to lose our trust,
In the Universal Good,
A void is created,
And the energy of death,
Springs forth,
Into our lives.

Sometimes it grasps us quickly,
Sometimes we allow it to seize us,
Slowly through disease,
As in a heart attack or stroke,
Does the energy of death,
Engulf our lives,
'Til life is gone,
And only death remains.

To experience the true,
Fullness of the energy of Life,
Let go.
Let go of
Frenzy
Aggression
Hatred and greed
Deceptiveness
Unforgiveness
Confusion
And find within yourself,
A pathway,
Back to,
Harmony
With the Universe.

RESTORE HONOR TO BUSINESS

Please reveal to me where honor has gone.
Please tell me why honoring one's word,
Is now measured in hours—perhaps minutes,
And breaking one's word,
Often occurs even faster.

Why does it seem impossible,
To base these affairs of business,
On a sense of unity,
And community;
On a sense of honor,
That reflects the needs of all?
Why does it always have to be,
Right now and my way?
Right now and my way and to hell with all the others.

Right now—my way—
Where has trust gone?
What has happened to understanding?
Humanness? Commitment to the long term?
Do we answer "they are all right—if
I can fill my pockets first?"
I try to take advantage of him,
He tries to take advantage of me,
I try to take advantage of him again.
Where does this all finally go?
Can we make a deal that is fair,
And long lasting,
With attitudes such as these?
What we build with such attitudes,
Is an unstable house of cards,
That at the flick of a finger,
Collapses into a pile of rubble.

Where does it truly finally go?
Where is honor?
Where is trust? Truth and balance?
What happened to understanding?
We started out to build a relationship,
That would endure;
That would withstand the slings and arrows,
That life would surely shoot at it.
Let's pray that we do not wind up,
With a house of cards,
That cannot even withstand,
The slightest puff of air.

If there is "honor among thieves,"
Should there be less than this,
Among men who do not steal?
For the sake of those concerned,
We must return to trust;
To cooperation—to truth—to balance—
We must return honor,
To the center of the deal.

SHODAN
(Karate)

In your essence,
I find
A sense of timelessness,
In which my masculinity grows.
In your loving discipline,
I am often one,
With Persifal
And Arthur
And all the others,
Who sat 'round that magnificent table,
And dedicated their soul,
To Honor
To Justice
And to Truth.

In you I find my strength,
My honor,
My meaning.
Through you I know an inner love of justice,
And of compassion for the weakness,
That lives in every man.
You are my guide,
You are my heart,
You are my spirit.
In your magnificent discipline,
I come to know,
What it truly means,
To be a man.

UNIVERSAL PROTECTION

When we feel fearful,
Empty
As though there is no one,
Or nothing on earth,
To protect us,
Trust.
Know that in the moment of feeling nothing,
There is everything.
The Universe protects those of its creatures,
Who cannot
Protect themselves.

NO GREATER GIFT

There is no greater gift,
That one can give a son,
Than freedom.

There is no greater blessing,
That can be bestowed upon him,
Than to place him,
In the care of God.

There is no greater feeling of security,
Than to know that he is here,
To be guided and protected,
By the Great Loving Intelligence
That created the universe.
After all—he was His son first.

WHEN I LOOK

A thing, a move, a simple act,
A collection of all three.
A waterfall,
A bouncing ball,
An evening by the sea.
A runner's stride,
A mountainside,
The wind that bends a tree.
A rainy night,
A sunrise bright,
A skater's symmetry.
In these, some may see just things,
But they are poetry for me.

TIDE

The tide is very high tonight,
It buffets rock and tree,
Its frothy fingers grip the beach,
Then retreat into the sea.

The ocean spans a distant mile,
Endless so it seems,
Man's ancient past is hidden there,
It drifts back in his dreams.

Clouds encase the mountain top,
In a veiled mystery,
The sun fades gently in the west,
God's perfect symmetry.

What great yet humble presence this,
The clouds, the tide, the sea,
Here a haunting billion years,
Before this poetry.

MAKING SENSE

Life oft is filled,
With making sense of things.
Mostly life dictates that things must be made sense of—
But often our thoughts,
May go awry,
And drift hither, there, everywhere,
In a remotely indecisive state,
Making little sense at all.

Frequently, however,
The best sense that can be made,
Is the sense that is made,
In this hour.
Now.

THE WAY

Sometimes I have a feeling,
That some of the things I do,
I was meant to do for many, many centuries.

Killing one person
Is as atrocious
As killing a million.

A DIVINE RESPLENDENCY

There is a Magnificent Resplendency,
That directs the affairs of men,
Whose loving voice repeats to all,
"Live this day the best you can."

Each man has within his mind,
An inner ear to hear,
To seek the message from this Source,
To make his path of life more clear.

Each man has within his heart,
A fountain of Its grace,
Sometimes silent—sometimes gushing,
Ebb and flow at human pace.

Each man has within his soul,
This capacity to be,
Thought-filled—loving—ever learning,
A divine resplendency.

There is the Presence of God in everyone.
Everyone
Everywhere.
If we could learn to express this Presence
there would be peace.

Suffering
unlocks the chains
that surround understanding and growth.

TIME

The present is elusive,
It is always becoming the past.
The future is always just becoming.
Tomorrow is an abstraction,
When it really comes it is today.
Yesterday is but a distant dream.
There is really only one time ever—
There is only now.

THIS INSTANT

I just want to be here,
In this time,
In this place,
In this experience.

Because now is the time for me to know,
That the past is ended.
Finally ended.

In this instant,
It is the glorious now—
And the future starts a moment later.

REUNION

I've been with you for a while,
Now, an inner voice tells me,
I must leave you and move on.
For deep within I know,
That life is not a station,
But a journey,
Toward an ever expanding dawn.

As I look from here the path seems long,
And winding,
And sometimes fraught with fear.
I'll miss your love and gentleness,
Your strength,
I'll long to have you near.

And when I stop along this path,
To rest my soul and heart,
With love, I'll look back there for you,
From whence I made my start.
You are not standing where you were,
Where you used to be;
You have taken your own path,
And have come very near to me.

(To my dear friend Fran Koehler)

CAST YOUR NETS
TO THE RIGHT

When things go wrong and problems mount,
And your thoughts are dismally bent,
And life seems to be—hopelessly,
By an evil siren sent.

Is this not what the fishermen thought,
At the Sea of Galilee?
They toiled long that night for nought,
Not a single fish did they see.

Then a carpenter from Galilee,
Came upon this dreary sight,
"Come with me," he said, "Go out again—
Cast your nets out to the right."

Now their nets were filled with powerful thoughts,
As they swept back out to sea,
His thoughts—and theirs blended fast,
To make a poignant mystery.

Though they never had this done before,
They cast their nets to the right,
And with the nets went the powerful thoughts,
Which filled them on that night.

To change your life—change your thoughts—
And you change your destiny;
Cast your nets out to the right,
And from problems you will be free.

OUR EMOTIONAL NATURE

A strong emotional nature,
Is like a great and powerful steed.
If you can control it,
It is a magnificent thing indeed.

You can ride it strongly,
Wherever you want to go,
To the top of any mountain,
Through wind or rain or snow.
Through the roughest country,
This magnificent steed will glide,
With speed and strength and energy,
If your reason is at its side.

If you master your emotional nature,
It will serve your every need,
Nurture it with spiritual thought,
An unconquerable steed—indeed!

Affirm the negatives in your life
and you really give them life.

A MAN'S IMMORTALITY

A man's full freedom comes in his perceptions of truth.
For when truth lights his understanding,
Error fades and dies,
And
As error after error drop away,
It is as though the clouds have parted,
And a glorious sunlight,
Reveals the magnificence of,
The new born day.
And in the expanding radiance of truth,
A man sees his soul,
And ultimate immortality.

LIFE

What is this stuff that fills my body
Called life?

Certainly it is of an essence more than the body,
For when it leaves what remains,
Turns quickly to clay.
It is love, I am sure, and hope,
And faith and gentleness.
It is happiness and kindness
And radiance and joy.

It is also often suffering, and fear
Anger and remorse.
Often grief.
But somehow these seem foreign,
To its pure essence;
For always there is a struggle,
To eliminate them,
As though they were alien,
And did not belong.

Life is a healthy body core,
Strength, acquisitiveness,
Intellectual power and integrity.
But most of all, life is hope and friendship,
And giving and caring,
Kindness and understanding,
Along with love, honesty, joy and tenderness.

Is life not the stuff of God?

ANOTHER WAY

I looked upon the traders pit,
And saw the mass below,
Of angry, shouting, grasping men,
Their tensions all aglow.

Up from this mixing, milling pit,
Arose a mournful cry,
Of tattered nerves and stress filled limbs,
And tensions, Oh, so high!

What was the frantic grand allure,
That kept those humans there,
Amid that hostile graspingness,
And angry shouts and blare?

Surely life is more than this,
I slowly came to see,
To watch a bird glide toward a rock,
With perfect symmetry.

To feel a breeze and watch a flower,
And hear the ocean roar,
To take a breath and sense the power,
Of a healthy body's core,
To come to know that life like this,
Is what the soul is yearning for.

THE ENDLESSNESS OF ME

I stood high upon an island,
Where the sea surrounds a volcanic core,
I watched the endless gentle wind,
Move the wavelets to the shore.

The sunlight danced upon these waves,
And as with an eternal brush,
Tinted each a golden hue,
Capped with diamond dust.

I stood upon this island,
And looked out upon the sea,
In one endless moment there,
I came to feel the beingness of me.

The endless sea, the endless sky,
The aged rock and shore,
Makes me know the meaning of,
My life as never before.

The sea extends in all directions,
The sky to infinity,
And in my heart I come to sense,
The endlessness of me.

MY TRUE POWER

There is a divine directing force within me,
Which seeks constantly to unfold;
It speaks to me only when I take the time,
In quietness to listen.

Very often, though, I am bombarded with,
The outer stimuli of life.
What to do today about a thing. . .
Another thing, another thing;
Who to see today about a fact. . .
Another fact, another fact;
What to do today about a problem. . .
Another problem, another problem;
Who to see today about a person. . .
Not looking at what is within, but the outer person.

When will my inner mind, in its magnificence,
Work for me?
I must seek first a realization,
Of my oneness with Immortal Mind.
And as I look within—deeply within,
To find this source
Then all things about the things,
All facts about the facts,
All solutions to life's problems,
All things about all persons,
Will be magnificently revealed to me.
And
As I look within,
Rather than to those outer things,
I unfold the true power of my life.

TRUE FREEDOM

Only the soul has the capacity,
To know true freedom.
It can search infinite distance,
And beyond this distance too,
Until once it senses the point of Pure Freedom,
It becomes light and love,
Infinity

Spend time with yourself—
That you may come to love the self you really are.

TEARS

It's a nice day when I can cry,
And release the inner fears,
That may have lived within my heart,
For many, many years.

Tears that come so slow at first,
Then with growing intensity,
Pull from deep within my being,
The spectre that troubles me.

Before tears came, my heart seemed bound,
By chains of deep adversity,
Once tears in full measure flow,
The chains are rent—tears set me free.

When I've cried and felt my grief,
My path becomes more clear,
My soul responds—uplifted, strong,
Life's course my hope can steer.

*(Dedicated to Elizabeth Jablonski who in a time of crisis, gave me the
opening line to this poem.)*

Tears wash away the cares of life
and leave us the salts of wisdom.

I HAD A DREAM

I had a dream,
That had a hidden meaning,
No—more of a little nightmare,
That tugged and pushed my emotions,
To and fro.

Although the dream,
Was frightening and confusing,
And bewildering,
I somehow "knew,"
That if I could find,
Its meaning,
Amid the fear, confusion,
And hidden innuendo,
A message would emerge,
That would become a pathway,
That when I walked upon it,
Would enhance my life.

NIGHT CHILD

Oh! Child of the night,
Child of fear and desolation,
This night what fiend-like phantom comes,
To threaten and torment you,
With fiery eyes and gnashing teeth,
To make your body cold and still,
With terror and trepidation?

Was that a voice?
Is someone there?
What was that creak?
That little noise—
That chills me with the,
Paralysis of impending doom,
And sends the hopelessness of fear,
Through me and the entire room.

I take a stand!
I say to you,
Fear not! Oh trembling little one.
Fear not! Oh child of the night.
Fear not I say to you!
I am here beside you now,
And here I shall ever be.

I'm here. And here I'll ever be.
To wrap my strength and love,
Around your trembling body fright,
And hold you safe,
And very close to me.
Fear not I say! Again I say,
Fear Not!
Till fear abates and trembling stops,
And quiet gently fills your soul.

—continued on page 56

55

Fear not! Fear not!
Oh anxious child of the night—
Fear not!
I am here to put to flight,
The threatening terror of this night,
To comfort you—
To stand as your protector bold,
To hold you safely in my arms,
Till gentle quiet comes,
And touches you,
And precious sleep enfolds.

(Dedicated to Marilyn Van Derbur Atler whose public declaration of being an abused child was the inspiration for this poem.)

TO MY DOG REX
Faithful Companion of My Youth

I now confront my grief.
I cannot believe that,
It has been over forty-five years,
Since you died,
Oh good and noble friend Rex,
My friend and the loving companion,
Of my youth.

When I needed love in those,
Troubled and unhappy times,
You were always there,
To wag your tail,
To lick my hand,
And I knew,
That no matter what thunderbolt,
Uncertain fate caused to strike near me,
You were there to love me,
Unconditionally.

You died only two days before,
I returned from serving in the
Pacific Fleet,
And I stuffed my grief,
And buried you without a tear.
So now the memory of your life with me,
Surges up from a forgotten place,
Somewhere deep within my mind.

—continued on page 58

I now shed the tears and face the grief,
That I could not shed and face,
Those many years ago,
When I covered you with earth,
In that shallow grave.

Now I grieve for you,
And shed my tears,
With wisdom and compassion,
I had not then;
And somewhere deep within my soul,
I know now,
That some day—somewhere,
In a future time of bliss,
We will meet again.

ACCEPTANCE

Maybe
The great lesson,
We can learn in life,
Is to come to understand and accept,
The role
The Universe has handed us.

AN ODE TO A SON
AND TO A FATHER

When you love,
I share your love.
When you are joyous,
My heart sings with you.

When you laugh,
I laugh with you.
When you triumph,
My spirit soars.

When you overcome,
I share the blessing of your triumphs.
Son, when you are strong,
I see my strength in you.

But if you are attacked,
I stand ever with you.
If defeat comes upon you,
I am defeated too.

If you feel sorrow,
My heart is heavy.
If you should suffer,
I suffer with you.
If you should shed your blood,
My blood flows too.
For
We are eternal companions,
Traveling in an indefinite world.
But one thing is definite,
I am always your father,
You are ever my son.

A SPIRITUAL FAMILY

A man and a woman,
From a different culture,
In a distant island,
Surrounded by the sea,
Came to visit other men and women,
In a place of many mountains,
With a different culture—far distant from the sea.

Despite the many miles and the differentness of cultures,
Which might have kept them separate and apart,
It became immediately apparent,
That they belonged to a single family,
A family of spirit—brothers and sisters all.
In those happy, joy filled hours when they met
An aura of understanding, warmth, and love,
Filled the hearts of every person there.

Now with blissful awareness,
The soul of each was touched by every other,
With wonderful compassion, warmth and tenderness;
And love so moved all present,
And filled their hearts with kindred feelings,
That it seemed they had known each other,
For a hundred thousand years.

And each, upon departing,
Knew they had enriched the lives,
Of those they met,
And were in turn enriched within their heart.
So now the land so distant from the ocean,
And the land of many mountains,
Are so filled with beauty from their presence,
That they will never,
Be quite the same again.

(Dedicated to Yasuhiko Sugiura and Rie Sandstrom whose visit to Denver deeply touched our hearts.)

WHO IS THIS MAN?

Who is this man?
He is neither tall nor short,
Not thin but slightly fleshy,
A man that is both an evil doer,
And a man easily led into evil.
A perfect artist,
To create things to meet his needs,
And to add his signature,
To the most terrible oaths,
To thus carry out his program.

How could this man fail,
To be some wicked demon,
Who must have been starved for love,
And many other things;
Who walked about the palace restlessly,
At unreasonable hours of the night,
Even though he was devoted,
To the joys of Aphrodite.

Who did not blush before,
Those destined to be ruined by him;
Who did not show anger or exasperation,
When his program was heavily thwarted;
Who would not relay his feelings,
To those who had offended him.

But with the quiet vindictiveness of a viper,
And with furrowed brow,
Would order the dismantling of cities,
The confiscation of possessions,
And monies from the treasury,
And who would order the death,

Of thousands of the innocent,
Both friend and foe alike.
And who became enraged,
And bared his teeth,
To those who tried to intercede,
Through prayers and supplications,
On behalf of those who had,
Offended him—
And would pardon not a single one of them.

And who was the cause,
Of countless calamities and deaths,
In the people of his country.
How many people have been destroyed,
And what disasters have occurred,
And starvations suffered,
By those who have survived his fury,
Is impossible to compute.

Who is this man?
Is it Justinian?
Is it Hitler?
Is it Stalin?
Saddam.

SOME COACHES

A group of thoughtless dunderheads,
Took the spirit of a boy,
And bent it down and twisted it,
As though it were a toy.

Though they professed to be his coach,
To help his confidence and pride,
They were concerned not with him at all,
Win! Win! their egos cried.

His spirit shook but did not break,
For he had a fighting heart,
He struggled with their sarcastic taunts,
Searching somehow for a new start.

So he took a bat and glove in hand,
In a game he scarcely knew,
And as he looked at me and I at him,
Both hope and anxiety grew.

Then he stepped into the batters box,
And tried with all his might,
And on the second pitch that day,
Drove a single out to right.

As days went on—in another game,
His confidence restored,
He hit the ball a distant mile.,
Into the street it soared!

He raised his arms triumphantly,
As he jogged home toward the plate,
They tried to break his spirit, but
He chose a different fate.

He now looks to life with hope,
His spirit on the mend,
With a lesson learned that dunderheads,
Are too dense to ever comprehend.

The Evolving Tao

Journey   Purpose   Path

A DIFFERENT WAY

When Life plants pitfalls
In our path
And there seems to be
A state of confusion
Everywhere,
It is only Life
Requesting
That we
Change our way.

GRACE

I thought
Life had cheated me.
It had not.
I came to see
Life had blessed me
All the way.

A WARRIOR'S LAST CALL

Today, Lord, I would rather
Be a poet,
Sitting in a high place,
Beside the sea;
Allowing my thoughts,
To drift
To those things of beauty,
In my life
And the lives of others—
Things of love and humanness,
And compassion and justice,
Things of the Spirit—and of the soul.

But you have chosen,
Another path for me, Lord.
You have called forth
Another energy—
And it comes forth.
So I put away the pen,
And I take down my armor,
And sword—
One more time,
To do those things,
That you have directed,
Me to do.

And I will do them,
With all the strength
Within me—
With all the inner fire,
And determination at my command.

—*continued on page 72*

One more time, Lord,
For as long as it takes,
To change the course,
To climb the wall,
To right the wrong,
To seek the new path,
And to accomplish these,
I now dedicate all my inner strength.

But I will miss,
The poetry—the words,
Of justice,
Love and compassion,
Of things human,
And of the Spirit,
That might have come to me,
While sitting in that high place,
By the sea.

A JOURNEY OF LOVE

Why don't you come
And be with me
On a journey
To the stars?
A journey of love,
Human love,
One human's love for another;
Whether it be,
A beautiful friendship,
Or an ecstatic love affair,
Or both,
For one often turns,
Into another.
Come be with me,
Lovingly
Forever
On a journey
To the stars.

ON THE JOURNEY OF LIFE

Each time
I gain a new understanding,
A new sense of knowing,
My life expands itself,
A little bit.
Every time I see a new truth,
The diamond of life,
Turns just a fraction,
And there is a new sparkle,
A new glitter,
A new radiance,
A new sense of the value,
Of being alive,
And a new realization,
That the journey of life,
And love,
Is indeed worthwhile.

The presence of God is always found,
On the winding pathway of love.

A TRANSITIONAL PRAYER

Infinite Father,
I place myself in your hands;
Where you send me,
I will go.
Where you guide me,
I will be directed.
When I think a thought,
Let it be your thought.
When I speak a word,
Let it be a word of friendship,
Or love.

Infinite Father,
I give you my mind,
My heart,
My soul.
Fill my consciousness with your love.
Guide me through this time,
Of trial and transition.

A FREE SPIRIT

Take a breath,
And look afar,
To a haunting, endless sea.

Stand alone,
On a star filled night,
And let your thoughts flow free.

The soul of man,
Was destined not,
For mundane captivity.
No power, dogma, rigid thought,
Can chain this mystery.

The spirit knows its source is God,
And reaches endlessly,
Breaking chains of any kind,
To find that destiny.

A VOICE FOR MEN TO HEAR

I pray
That God will give me,
Through these lines,
And others,
That I have written,
A voice that men,
Will hear.

For the age has come,
In the history of men,
When they should begin,
To understand,
And come into a new awakening,
Of sensitive thoughts,
And feelings,
And recognize the beauty of Spirit,
Within their souls.

And in their lives,
Come to know,
Tenderness
Understanding
Kindness and joy—
And learn to express,
These inner feelings,
As a part of their beings.

WHAT IS THE PURPOSE?

As I sit beside the sea and reflect upon my life,
I come to know there is a part of me that is a hopeless striver,
Struggling, stressing endlessly it seems,
Like the hopeless sandcrab making his way up the coral rock,
Surging forward—slipping backward—surging forward,
A grain of sand or two move under his claws—
And he loses ground ten times his height—
Straining upward, onward 'til upon nearly reaching the top,
A giant wave,
Comes forth and carries him backward again.
If he is a creature of the sea,
Would his purpose not be better served,
By riding the crest of the wave to the top?

I look upon a beach and see a rock and wonder what is the purpose
of the rock?
Is it there just by chance, aimlessly?
I look upon the ocean and wonder what is the purpose of the ocean?
Is it there simply to pound upon the shore endlessly?
I look upon a tree swaying in the breeze and again I wonder,
What is its purpose?'
Is it simply there to be a tree in nothingness?
I look upon a bird gliding across a bay to a distant rock.
What is its purpose? Simply to exist?
I look upon a man and see him endlessly scurrying about,
Pushing this—moving that—adjusting this—
Is this his purpose?
Then I look upon myself,
Sometimes apprehensive about things,
Often concerned about the acts of people—the fundamentals of a
situation.

—continued on page 80

I ask myself, "Why can't things go as I would have them go?"
And then like the sand crab pushing up the jagged coral rock,
I begin to strive and push and slip and slide,
And sand erodes beneath my grasp,
And I feel myself slipping ten times my height.

There are other times when I look out upon the sea,
And listen to the wind slip through the trees,
And watch a flower bend gently in the breeze,
It is then I seem to know there is a greater purpose.
There is a purpose in the rock.
There is a purpose in the sea.
There is a purpose in a man.
There is a purpose in the tree.
There is a far greater purpose in life for me.
And in times like these I know that my life has infinite meaning.

When I place my life in the hands of the Eternal Intelligence,
That knows each and every purpose—
That knows the reason the rock rests quietly upon the beach,
The reason the sea moves endlessly against the jagged shore,
The reason the tree sways gently in a never ending breeze,
The reason that the bird flies and man strives.
When I place my concerns, hopes and desires in the care of this magnificent,
Loving Intelligence—without hesitation and with total trust—
Then I understand my life and my purpose.

A UNIVERSAL WIND

I sat upon a mountain top,
And looked up to the stars,
I felt alone because I seemed to see,
My sight was reaching God.

While I looked upon this vast,
Magnificent display,
I sensed a thread that was not there,
Yet there in every way.

A Universal Wind was there,
Among the stars and galaxies,
A Wind that threaded through them all,
And moved them perfectly.

I saw each planet, sun and moon,
Threaded in its place,
By that unseen Wind that moved throughout,
The infinity of space.

I looked afar and came to know,
That Wind was always there,
No beginning; never ending,
Filled with hope and care.

As I sent my thoughts afar out there,
Beyond the galaxies,
I gleaned a truth that I shall treasure,
Always—endlessly.

I came to know that it was there,
An eternity ago,
The Loving Wind that placed me here,
Was always there for me to know.

Unconditional Love

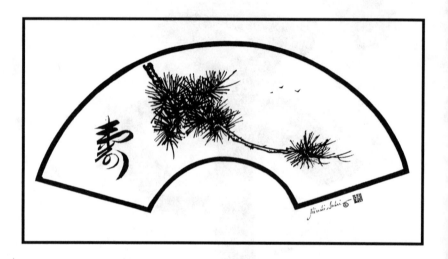

UNCONDITIONAL LOVE

The knowledge and deep feeling,
That I have experienced,
An unconditional love from you,
Soul to Soul,
Many, many times,
Made me able to,
Understand and tell you,
Of this ecstatic, frightening,
Joyous experience;
Confusing and frustrating at first,
But later filled with trust,
And with great confidence,
In my love for others,
And especially for you.

I share this with you,
Because
I would like to help you know,
What I have seen,
With the eye of my soul,
Without perhaps as much,
Of the frustration, anxiety,
And sometimes stomach numbing fear,
That I felt as I walked the winding pathway,
To this beautiful discovery.

TO KNOW LOVE

There is love.
There is joy.
There is hope.
There is happiness.
There is strength.
There is courage.
There is devotion to duty too.
There is anger.
There is fear.
There is resentment sometimes,
But forgiveness erases this from the soul.
Forgiveness is blissful,
It fills us with joy,
But it is greater for us to know love.

LOVE IS AN ACT

A word, a blush, a loving touch,
A combination of the three.
A flower sent,
With fond intent,
A card that says, "Love Thee."
A kiss that's blown,
A smile shown,
An embrace to feel and see;
A gentle hand that reaches out,
When your heart needs sympathy.
Love's someone to miss,
It's a lover's kiss,
It's a song—a symphony.
It's a warm caress,
It's someone you bless,
And wish prosperity.
Now with these thoughts,
My spirit soars,
They make my heart just sing,
Love is giving, feeling—reaching out,
Love is an act—it's not a thing.

(To my daughter, Liz, whose love inspired these lines.)

LOVE IS A VERB

Love's a soft spoken word,
To someone you enjoy,
Love's a hug and a kiss,
For a sad little boy.

Love's a call on a night,
When someone's feeling down,
Love is help and advice,
When confusion surrounds.

Love's a signal that says,
You're my very best friend,
Love's the sadness you feel,
When the evening must end.

Love's an act, not a thing,
Love is bliss spread around,
Love is deep feelings shared,
In which lovers abound.

My soul sings with delight,
At these thoughts so profound,
My heart soars—filled with joy,
Love's a verb—not a noun.

(To my son, Steve)

I DID IT MY WAY

This is a poem,
I needed to write—
A sonnet,
I needed to speak—
About human love,
One person for another.

So I spoke it,
Gently, I hoped,
With compassion—
I told her I loved her;
Oh—not in so many words,
But my message of love,
For her,
Was there none the less.

It was nothing that was physical,
Or glamorous,
Nothing clinging,
Nothing binding or romantic,
No projections,
Or illusions.

Just that I loved her,
Because I could so clearly see,
The radiant,
Presence of God,
Within her,
As she sat there,
Across the table,
From me.

IS IT BETTER?

Is it better to say you care . . .
Than to truly care
And send a bouquet of flowers?

EACH SPRING

Each spring,
When the days grow slowly longer,
And the sun gently warms my face;
When the smell of blooming lilacs,
Stimulates my thoughts and memories;
When the first happy notes of the returning birds,
With their haunting melodies arouse,
Deep sensations of love,
Within my soul.

When the pungent smell of new leaves,
And the radiance of the tulips,
Bring back memories of the ecstasy,
We felt,
In those exciting days,
In that enchanting spring,
When we fell,
So deeply,
In love.

ANIMA

You are to me,
A star deep in outer space,
And a flame deeper than that,
In the center of my being.

For me you are the sense,
Of always having been,
And the bliss,
Of never ending, too.

Your beauty,
Lights a fire in my soul,
And then that beauty,
Is reflected back to me.

Your love lifts my spirit,
To untold heights,
And
In my love for you,
There was never a beginning,
And
There can never be an end.
Never.
And forever.

SOUL MATE

It came to me in a dream,
A few nights ago,
A dream that gave my mortal mind,
A freedom to see beyond the lock,
Of my contemporaneous body—
A dream that opened a door,
And revealed the long, long pathway,
We have journeyed—
And in an instant,
I saw the million years,
That our souls have traveled together.

When I awoke,
It was as though my whole being,
Was lifted to,
A magnificent sense of ecstasy,
Wonderment,
And bliss—
And in those short moments,
I lived a million years with you.

Now as I write these lines,
I feel again that sense of bliss,
Joy,
Ecstasy,
And love for you.

—continued on page 94

I've now lived a moment,
That few men have ever lived—
And during that moment,
I came to know,
That our souls have been joined,
Oh! So many times;
In that moment,
I found you,
Soul mate.

AN AWAKENING

I have such warm and gentle feelings for you,
I think I could learn to love you unconditionally,
And I would like to try—when and if,
Your life permits this.

This is what I meant to say,
When I sent that flower,
On that day so long ago—
Or so it seems so long ago.
I didn't understand then,
What my inner self spoke so clearly to me,
Just a few short moments ago—
I can now admit the thought of this,
Fills me with great warmth and joy.

Although my ego says,
"Stop—right now! Do not go on!"
A purer thought from deep within my soul,
Says to me "Beautiful feelings of this kind,
Come to you so seldom,
That the object of this warmth and joy,
Should know this,
Despite how vulnerable they make you feel."

And so in this frightening openness,
I send you this message,
To do with it,
What your heart and spirit direct.

I MUST MOVE ON

I thought that I could come to love you,
But now my weary heart,
Tells me,
That I must move on.

I thought that I could come to you,
And lay my weary head,
Upon your breasts,
And have you caress,
My brow,
By laying gentle hands,
Upon me.

But despite the little signs I get from you,
And the messages of love I've sent,
Something within you,
Kept you from acknowledging,
My message of commitment and love.

And you know well that my journey,
Cannot be delayed,
By your need right now,
To tarry,
With games of fear and caprice,
Which make my heart sad,
And still my love,
So very, very quiet.

My soul weeps—it cries aloud
To find another,
With deeper sensitivity,
And openness,
With ears to hear the song of love,
That I have sent to you.

But you saw none of this,
And there was nothing I could do,
To open your eyes—
So,
In sorrow,
For the beauty that could have been,
My heart tells me,
That now I must move on.

Because of you,
In this lifetime,
I need never love again.

The capacity to love unconditionally,
Brings unconditional love.

THE LIGHT OF LOVE

Love is the presence within us,
That lights our way.
Love is the presence that will,
Ultimately perfect itself.
Often, in this day, it is a gem,
That is covered by refuse—
A pearl that is tread upon by swine—
Only sometimes gleaming,
Through the muck of living,
But there—nonetheless—radiant,
And beautiful—ready to surface.
The refuse in no way diminishes,
The essence of the diamond.
The mud does not alter,
The true beauty of the pearl.
The diamond and the pearl,
Symbolize our great capacity,
For loving expression—
For beautiful words, deeds—and feelings.
This capacity is there in all humankind,
Especially in the soul of woman.
Mud and refuse cannot permanently dull this light—
Ultimately it will show through.
It will illuminate our every act,
Until the path is clear,
And the way made radiant by the light of love.

LOVE YOU FROM A DISTANCE

I fell in love with you,
The first time I saw you,
On that rainy night in March,
A year ago.

My going back to find you,
Was, I thought, an act of futility,
I never dreamed that I'd see you again.
Just when I felt I'd lost you,
You appeared behind me—
How does one explain,
This haunting mystery?

I tried hard to avoid my feelings,
I said they were not important,
And went about my life mechanically.
How could such a beautiful woman,
So young and vivacious,
Be interested in an older man?

But when you called me that evening,
You sent a loving message,
Which opened the gateway,
That I had closed tightly,
On my love.

I slowly came to realize,
That I had not had such feelings,
In what seems,
To be a thousand years—or so.

—continued on page 102

I'm enchanted by what happened,
In this loving revelation,
That has filled my heart,
With happiness and joy.
Because I found that I could love you,
For the simple joy of loving,
Even if forever,
We remained a thousand miles apart.

And if nothing further happens,
And we never come together,
My love for you,
Will forever fill my heart.

Something that everyone dreams of. . .
To be loved unconditionally.

KINDRED SPIRIT

Distant lights are twinkling brightly,
Much like diamonds in the sea.
Distant wavelets moving gently,
Toward the shore, Lo! Come to me.

As we live this mystic moment,
It is as it will ever be,
For our souls have loved each other,
In other ages by the sea.

If there was another living
In a distant life ago
Surely our lips came together,
Yea, my heart knows this is so.

Tonight we feel our hearts united,
And our love does blend and be,
Again together for this moment,
On our path toward immortality.

Love is like a ray of light;
It can go far into the universe,
And deep into the soul.

SOMETIMES SOUL MATES
DO NOT MEET

Sometimes soul mates do not meet.
Sometimes they touch for just a moment,
And as they touch,
They reflect on what they see,
Of the other's exterior self.

If one's vision is clouded,
By exterior appearance alone,
Not meeting becomes very easy.
He is not instantly perfect—
He's a little bit too short—
Or much too tall—
He's too heavy or not heavy enough—
His smile is really "just not like . . ."

She has a different smile—
Blonde—not brunette—
Perhaps a little taller—
Or thinner—
Or shorter—
With blue green eyes—
Not brown—
So the thought comes easily,
"This one can't be the one."

Is there a beauty undetected?
A wonderfully vibrant essence,
At a soul-depth not perceived?
Can strength and warmth,
And caring,
Be so subtly hidden,
That they pass,
Before our very eyes?

Not him.
He's not instantly perfect—
A bit too tall or heavy—
Or too short—
Or not my type—
With brown eyes—
She wanted blue—
This must not be he.

She has a different smile—
Blonde and not brunette—
Perhaps a little taller—
Or thinner—
Or shorter—
With brown eyes not green—
Oh this cannot be she.

So we touch for just that moment,
Then our life paths,
Move apart,
Not to know in this lifetime,
The true meaning of our heart.
Sometimes soul mates do not meet.

A MEMORY

Sometimes,
The memory of you,
Drifts back to me. . .

I see a neckline,
A back,
Lovely hair,
And when the face turns,
So I can see it full,
It is not you. . .
My heart is touched,
The love's still there.

Sometimes,
The memory of you,
Drifts back to me. . .

Learn to be vulnerable.
There is a chance for hurt. . .
But there is also a chance for love.

Love is like a flower. . .
It grows best in the sunshine of understanding.

Nature

Beauty   Regeneration   Wholeness

CHRYSALIS

A caterpillar crawls,
Along the railing of a porch,
In a kind of ignorant serenity.
Only slightly does he sense,
There's a butterfly essence,
In a metamorphosis that will come to be.

As a caterpillar moves,
In his sinuous, halting creep,
His whole substance tuned to earth—not sky;
In the fabric of his being,
God's miraculous foreseeing,
He has a butterfly's capacity to fly!

The caterpillar reflects,
What we often suspect,
That a miracle in us can take place too.
Our catalyst is thought,
Something caterpillars have not,
With ascendant thinking we our miracle can view.

Surely we can see,
From our mundane captivity,
That the butterfly was God's transcendent hue;
This truth we must glean,
From deep within our being,
That God's metamorphosis, for us is equally true.

A FLOWER

A universe that creates a flower,
We can surely trust.
Its radiant beauty—graceful splendor,
From a loving cosmos thrust.

But a flower was not sent to be,
A common, ephemeral thing,
With fleeting beauty, comely grace,
Just a child of the spring.

The ethereal thought that shaped the mold,
Of petal, leaf and stem,
Was encompassed by a greater thought,
Concerned with lives of men.

The universe expressed the flower,
So we could come to see,
That like the flower, we too express,
An infinite resplendency.

BEAUTY

Physical beauty can be,
Both a blessing and a curse—
A two edged sword—
For
Outer beauty can sometimes,
Be so dazzling,
That its glitter,
Dyes the inner workings,
Of the soul.

Outer beauty
Is transient—
It's there and then
It is gone.

Outer beauty must be,
Accompanied,
By inner beauty—
Treasures of love,
Stored in the heart,
And soul.

Outer radiance of body,
Should be a reflection,
Of inner love of others,
And of one's self—
Of selfless love—
And humility.
So at the time in life,
When outer beauty fades,
The radiance of beauty,
Stored within,
Shines forth,
As a triumphant replacement.

The dawn leaves me
with a sense of new creation—
everywhere.

A SEARCH FOR WHOLENESS

There is in every human being,
A great,
And pressing need,
For wholeness.

Wholeness of mind,
Body and spirit,
Is very hard to find,
And requires great effort.
Sometimes it is fleeting,
We glimpse its splendor—
Then it is gone.

When it comes to us,
In understanding,
It fills our soul,
With immeasurable joy.

There are times when it comes,
Only as a feeling,
That often leaves us breathless,
But always filled,
With blissful awareness.

Many try to find wholeness,
In the outer things in life.
In possessions,
Of one type or another,
In other people,
Intoxicants,
Including food and drugs.

—continued on page 118

It is never there—
Not in these outer things in life.

For it is not what we own,
Or what we put within ourselves,
That leads to inner growth,
But what we find,
As we search,
Among the frightening inner pathways,
To the soul,
That causes the pain,
Of inner search,
To become,
An infinite reward.

A SUNSET

There is a mystery in the sunset.
The beautiful fire turns into gentle warmth,
Then fades into the sea.

I see the sunset in you,
From passionate burning,
To gentle beauty,
A graceful tenderness,
Not around you,
Or beside you,
But within you,
There I see the sunset.
And at this moment,
In its fire and warmth,
I see so clearly,
The radiant presence,
Of God within you.

A dream is a vision not yet realized.

SNOW

When the first snow of winter falls,
Memories stir in me,
Poignant, loving, bittersweet,
As the past can only be.

Days of my youth. . .in a far-removed place,
Flowing back through me,
Memories of fear and death and sorrow,
Lack and poverty.
As I look upon the fallen snow,
I am filled with gratitude.
I know a mysterious loving Source,
Led me through that interlude.

Snow reminds me of a rugged start,
And a determined persistency,
Strong thoughts from days gone by,
That changed life and circumstance for me.

Snow also brings me happy thoughts,
Of warm evenings by the sea,
Of sunny isles and loving times,
With people close to me.

But most of all—when snow does fall,
I sense a mystery,
Feelings come into my soul,
As a dream long past for me.

This much I know—from winter snow,
That I shall always be,
Searching, striving on my path,
Toward immortality.

Death

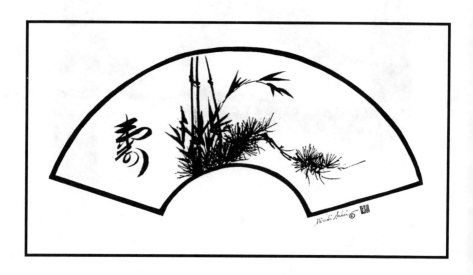

THE ULTIMATE REALITY

There are no rocks,
There are no rills,
There are no flowers,
Or distant hills,
There are no songs of sad lament,
There are no words of discontent,
There are no things of "you" or "I,"
There are no birds up in the sky,
These things you leave here when you die.

There is only spirit.
Immortal soul.
Death brings the ultimate reality.

(To my sister, Betty, whom I loved greatly.)

I FREE THEE
(and me)

I suffer loss—I feel the hurt,
That only death can bring.
Death—Death,
You grip my being,
You rend my heart, my love is gone,
You've taken her from me.

My grief is deep,
My soul is sad,
From you I must be free.
I write a poem to free my soul,
To cause my tears to flow,
To send my loved one's spirit on.

Spirit—Spirit,
Pause a while,
Send back your love to me.
Hear this verse I wrote for you,
To free myself and thee—
Hear and bless and understand,
How much you meant to me.

I hope that when my time arrives,
To leave and join thee,
Someone will write a verse like this,
My soul to also free;
To send it gently on its path,
With hallowed poetry.

TO MY GRANDMOTHER
(A Soliloquy)

They buried some of my soul with her,
That dismal, dreary day,
They lowered it into the earth,
And covered it with clay.

She used to make the day so bright,
And filled with happiness,
Her gentle warmth—her loving touch,
A tender, soft caress.

She gave me her love— her strength—her heart,
So very endlessly,
Now her soul I try to cast,
In this soliloquy.

She did her best to fight it off,
To live to be with me,
I prayed so hard to change the course,
Of her spirit's destiny.

But Something more than both of us,
Had the final say,
So now my soul is less in me,
They covered it with clay.

GRANDMOTHER
(A Revelation)

I crushed the weeds beneath my feet,
As I walked away that day,
Her unconditional love was gone,
They'd covered it with clay.

Her love had meant so much to me,
My heart it warmed and filled,
I longed again to have her near.,
Her love by death was stilled.

Barren thoughts and barren words,
Grief then filled my life,
In the near and in the far,
Life's path was filled with strife.

What could replace this glorious love,
That now was cold and still?
Delving—probing—searching for,
The void somehow to fill.

From boy to man I toiled life's path,
And came to understand,
Her love by death could not be stilled,
It transcended clay and sand.

A spirit warm and filled with love,
I slowly came to see,
Cannot be robbed by death's cold hands,
Of its loving immortality.

Lo, like the sun that from afar,
Sends forth its radiant light,
Her spirit once more sends it love,
My soul again is bright.

TASHA
(A Remembrance)

Love was the only purpose in her life,
This she did until the day she died,
Her love for us was unconditional,
She was always at our side.

There were moments when she irked us,
As dogs will sometimes do,
Tasha's hair is everywhere—we said,
And this was true.

But when we left our house at night,
Or when we went to sleep,
She was there to watch and guard,
Our safety her's to keep.

Always when I reached my home,
Before my foot could touch a stair,
Her nose would peak around a door,
Or poke from behind a chair.

Now—when I first come through my door,
I almost always think I'll see,
Her there somewhere in the house,
Peering gently up at me.

While death has taken her from us,
Her love for us complete,
Her spirit lives within these walls,
And in our hearts replete.

EXPECTATION

With the fear of death,
There comes the expectation,
To live new life—
To watch the leaves come forth
And the tulips blossom.

With the expectation of death,
There comes,
An energy for renewal—
An energy that fills the soul,
With the warmth of regeneration.

CONFRONTATION

I have come to grips with,
Death a hundred times,
And more than this,
Do I face death's energy,
Each day.

Every time I'm
Confronted
With the temptation to lie,
Or cheat
Or speak a falsehood of another—

Every time I face the trial of,
Deception
Greed
Hatred
Or unforgiveness—

When I choose not,
To love
To forgive
To honor my sister,
And my brother—

Then
At the very instant,
I face
One of these,
I come to a confrontation,
With the energy
Of death.

Sometimes we forget
Something we know deep inside ourselves. . .
It is that
All life dies and lives again.

AT DEATH

You were in this place for a while,
Now your spirit says it must move on,
With a smile—after looking back a moment,
You move toward the glory of the dawn.

For life is a journey, not a station,
A journey which the spirit takes to see,
Love and hope and friendship,
Sometimes sorrow—often complexity.

Surely now you know the meaning,
Of the essence spirit seeks to be,
And you have gone a little further,
In your path toward God—infinity.

Though you precede me in this journey,
Your purpose in this life complete,
Know—that when I complete my journey,
Our spirits once again shall meet.

A JOURNEY

Ah, Death is but a release and a remembering,
Of the freedom inherent in the soul—
When Spirit is unshackled from the body,
It can again focus on its majestic goal.

For the body is but an earthly prison,
In which the Spirit is tested morally—
After life's adversities have shaped it,
Spirit wends again toward its destiny.

For a moment life's trials are remembered,
Then spirit moves on joyfully—
Alas, earth's trials were but a hindrance,
On its journey toward God—Eternity.

DEATH

Ah, Death, you black and ugly mask,
So final, so unyielding, so bleak.
Do you control unquestionably man's days and nights forever?
Do you reach out and touch the flesh of man eternally?
Is it in your power that you should speak and man obey—
As though his spirit was not a force above you?
Are you ever unconquerable and unchallenged?
Until man questions your authority, he remains,
Ever victim to your power.
Ultimately you shall release the onerous grasp,
You have upon him.
Alas, his infinite spirit transcends you now,
As does his soul immortal.
Only mortal mind and mortal flesh now establish your reality.
One day a splendid metamorphosis shall take place,
When mind unites with spirit,
And with the soul,
And ultimately your grasp upon the body,
Must be released
To the magnificent power of this transcendent coalescence.
Man then becomes the master of his mortal fate
And your onerous grasp upon him is destroyed forever.

EPILOGUE

Creative mystics were ever a cross for the Church, but it is to them that we owe what is best in humanity.

Carl Jung-Mysterium Coniunctionis

The poetry you have just read emerged, sometimes with emotional pain and suffering, from the inner reaches of my unconscious mind. While writing these poems, I often became so absorbed in their content that I was almost completely unaware of my conscious thoughts or the outer things that surrounded me. This suppression of conscious thought was vitally important. It allowed access to the unconscious mind, which is almost always an ideational source necessary for the process of growth and the expression of the whole personality.

It is a relatively common misconception that the conscious mind possesses complete control over our thoughts, that what science calls the "psyche" is confined to the gray matter within our skulls; but as Carl Jung so brilliantly asserted "the psyche is rather a door that opens upon the human world from a world beyond, allowing unknown and mysterious powers to act upon humans and carry them on the wings of the night to a more personal destiny."* While it was not originally thus intended, accessing these powers became one of the salient efforts of this poetry.

* Source: *Psychological Reflections*. Jacobi, J., & Hull, .R.F... Bollingen Series XXXI. 1970, Princeton University Press, Princeton, .N.J. p. 320.

I deeply hope that the thoughts and insights I attempted to convey have emotional and spiritual value for you. I admit serious debate with myself about the thought of sharing these highly personal feelings and experiences. Considering the possible consequences of this sharing, created an apprehension of considerable magnitude for me. While the fear of self-revelation lurks deep in nearly all of us, this condition may have been greater for me than for most, because admittedly, earlier in my life I had so little to give.

I have now come to realize, however, that fear and trepidation are necessary parts of the process of "giving back"—of returning to others the benefit of the lessons life has taught me. In this act of giving, I am fully aware that I have made extensive revelations about myself—and that it is necessary that these revelations be given to others in totality; to release them to others to claim them as their own. In the act of total release there is always a sense of loss and I freely admit that this process has caused me to experience loss; however, when looked at in a different way, there is also a spirited sense of gain—for loss cannot be experienced unless that which is lost is believed to have value. It is in this atmosphere that I have submitted the content of this poetry to you.

Finally, after having shared these many thoughts and experiences, I would now like to take a moment to wish you a blissful life and blessings of great magnitude. May your path be filled with joy and happiness, and when difficult times come—as they most assuredly will—may you find in them lessons of increased awareness and spiritual understanding.